DOGS AT WORK

SLED DOGS

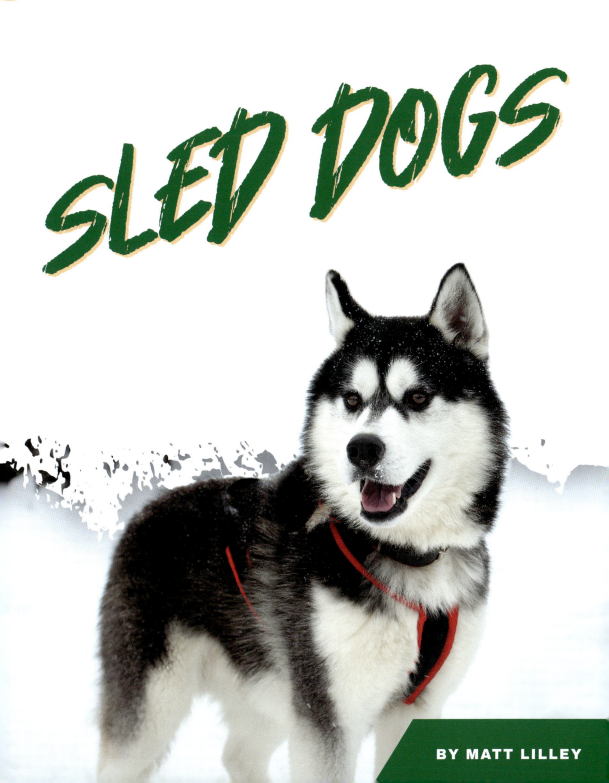

BY MATT LILLEY

WWW.APEXEDITIONS.COM

Copyright © 2023 by Apex Editions, Mendota Heights, MN 55120. All rights reserved. No part of this book may be reproduced or utilized in any form or by any means without written permission from the publisher.

Apex is distributed by North Star Editions:
sales@northstareditions.com | 888-417-0195

Produced for Apex by Red Line Editorial.

Photographs ©: Shutterstock Images, cover, 4–5, 6–7, 10–11, 12, 13, 14–15, 18–19, 20–21, 24, 25, 26–27, 29; iStockphoto, 1, 8, 16–17, 22–23; AP Images, 9

Library of Congress Control Number: 2022912282

ISBN
978-1-63738-426-8 (hardcover)
978-1-63738-453-4 (paperback)
978-1-63738-506-7 (ebook pdf)
978-1-63738-480-0 (hosted ebook)

Printed in the United States of America
Mankato, MN
012023

NOTE TO PARENTS AND EDUCATORS

Apex books are designed to build literacy skills in striving readers. Exciting, high-interest content attracts and holds readers' attention. The text is carefully leveled to allow students to achieve success quickly. Additional features, such as bolded glossary words for difficult terms, help build comprehension.

TABLE OF CONTENTS

CHAPTER 1
Over Ice and Snow 4

CHAPTER 2
From the Far North 10

CHAPTER 3
Ready to Pull 16

CHAPTER 4
Learning the Ropes 22

COMPREHENSION QUESTIONS • 28
GLOSSARY • 30
TO LEARN MORE • 31
ABOUT THE AUTHOR • 31
INDEX • 32

CHAPTER 1

OVER ICE AND SNOW

It's winter in Alaska. The air is freezing cold. A team of dogs run across the snow. They are pulling a sled.

Sled dogs can run far in cold weather. Their thick fur keeps them warm.

The dogs reach a frozen river. The **musher** on the sled yells, "On by!" The dogs pull the sled onto the ice. They race to the other side.

FAST FACT

On by is a mushing **command**. It means "keep going."

Sled dogs can run more than 25 miles (40 km) in one day.

When running long distances, sled dogs take breaks. They rest in beds of straw.

The dogs run for hours. Then they stop to rest. The next day, the dogs keep going. They run and pull the sled many miles.

A FAMOUS RUN

In 1925, sled dogs brought medicine to sick people in Nome, Alaska. Several dog teams worked together. One team ran more than 260 miles (418 km). Their work saved many lives.

A deadly disease spread near Nome, Alaska, in 1925. Several dog teams brought medicine there quickly.

CHAPTER 2

FROM THE FAR NORTH

People have used sled dogs for thousands of years. Dogs first pulled sleds in the Arctic. They helped **Indigenous** people travel and haul loads.

The Chukchi people of northeastern Siberia have used sled dogs for many years.

Sled dogs remain important to many Indigenous **cultures**. The Chukchi, Nenets, and Inuit are some of them.

The Inuit of North America have bred several types of sled dogs.

Samoyeds are descendants of dogs raised by the Nenets.

FAST FACT

Common sled dog **breeds** include the Siberian husky, the Alaskan malamute, and the Samoyed.

People also compete in dogsled races. Speed races are often 3 to 30 miles (5–48 km) long. Long-distance races can last many miles. Some take more than a week to run.

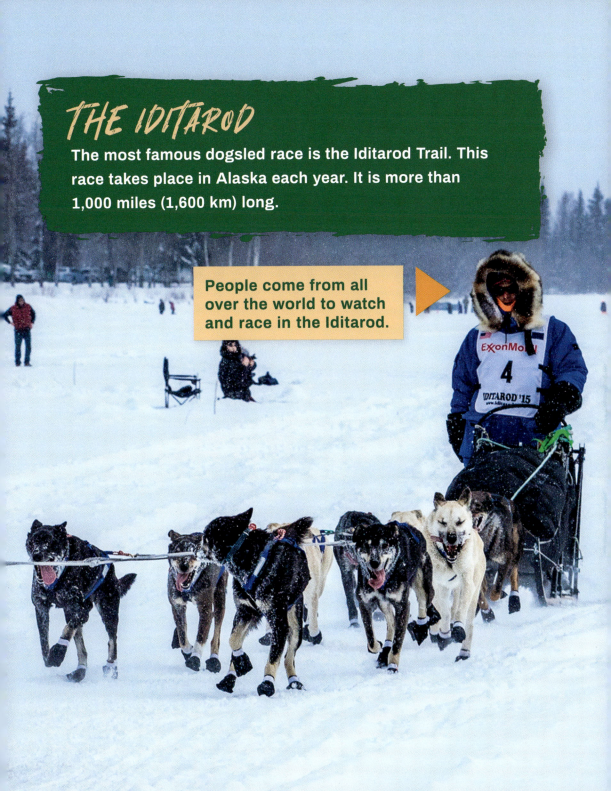

THE IDITAROD

The most famous dogsled race is the Iditarod Trail. This race takes place in Alaska each year. It is more than 1,000 miles (1,600 km) long.

People come from all over the world to watch and race in the Iditarod.

CHAPTER 3

READY TO PULL

Sled dogs work on teams. Each dog wears a **harness**. Ropes attach the dogs' harnesses to the sled.

One long rope runs down the middle of the team. Smaller ropes connect to each dog's harness.

Dogs on a team have different jobs. Wheel dogs are closest to the sled. They help turn the sled, so they must be big and strong. Team dogs are in the middle. They **maintain** the sled's speed.

FAST FACT
A sled dog team often has between 4 and 16 dogs.

Bigger sleds often have several pairs of team dogs.

All sled dogs must run fast and pull hard.

Lead dogs run at the front. They set the **pace** and direction for the other dogs. They listen for the musher's commands.

KEEPING IN STEP

Sled dogs run in pairs. Dogs of similar sizes often run together. That way, their **strides** match. This makes the ride smoother.

CHAPTER 4

LEARNING THE ROPES

Sled dogs start training as puppies. First, they get used to wearing harnesses. Then they learn to pull.

A sled dog's harness helps it pull heavy loads safely.

Younger dogs are often paired with older dogs to help them learn.

Young dogs start by pulling something light, such as a small sled. Then they learn to work with other dogs. They practice pulling as a team.

FAST FACT
Some dogs do skijoring. They pull people on skis.

In skijoring, a dog's harness connects to a belt worn by a person.

Sled dogs also learn commands. Mushers yell these words as the dogs run. During training, mushers give their dogs treats. They reward the dogs for each correct response.

Mushers start training their dogs many months before they race.

MUSHING COMMANDS

Mushers say *hike* to tell the dogs to start moving. *Gee* means to turn right. *Haw* means to turn left. *Easy* means slow down. *Whoa* means stop.

COMPREHENSION QUESTIONS

Write your answers on a separate piece of paper.

1. Write a paragraph that explains the main ideas of Chapter 2.

2. Would you want to compete in a dogsled race that was many days long? Why or why not?

3. Which mushing command means to start moving?

   A. hike
   B. gee
   C. have

4. Which type of dog is the farthest from the sled when the team runs?

   A. lead dog
   B. team dog
   C. wheel dog

5. What does **haul** mean in this book?

Dogs first pulled sleds in the Arctic. They helped Indigenous people travel and haul loads.

    A. take apart
    B. break or stop
    C. move or carry

6. What does **reward** mean in this book?

During training, mushers give their dogs treats. They reward the dogs for each correct response.

    A. show anger
    B. feel very sad
    C. give a gift or treat

Answer key on page 32.

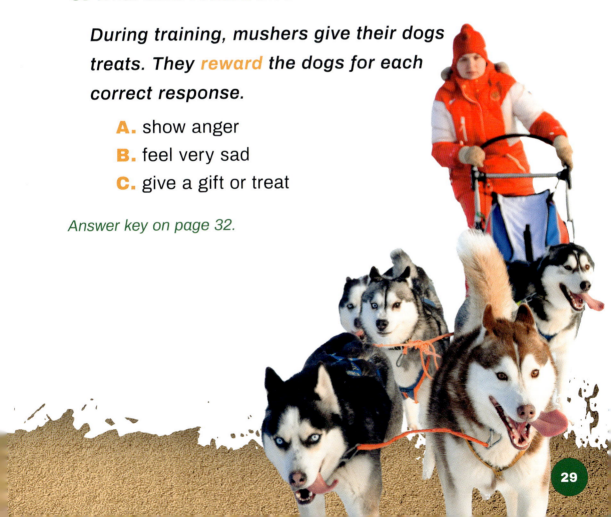

GLOSSARY

breeds
Specific types of dogs that have their own looks and abilities.

command
A way of telling a dog what to do.

cultures
Groups of people and the ways they live, including their beliefs and laws.

harness
A set of straps that attach a dog to a sled.

Indigenous
Related to the original people who lived in an area.

maintain
To keep something the same.

musher
A person who rides on a dogsled and guides the dogs.

pace
How fast something or someone moves.

strides
Steps, or the speed and size of those steps.

TO LEARN MORE

BOOKS

Berne, Emma Carlson. *Balto*. New York: Scholastic Press, 2022.

Klepeis, Alicia Z. *Sled Racing Dogs*. Minneapolis: Abdo Publishing, 2019.

Pearson, Marie. *Dog Trainer*. North Mankato, MN: Capstone Press, 2019.

ONLINE RESOURCES

Visit **www.apexeditions.com** to find links and resources related to this title.

ABOUT THE AUTHOR

Matt Lilley has an MS in scientific and technical writing. The focus of his degree was on medical writing for kids. He loves researching and writing about all sorts of topics. He lives in Minnesota with his family.

INDEX

A
Alaska, 4, 9, 15
Alaskan malamute, 13
Arctic, 10

C
Chukchi, 12
commands, 7, 21, 26–27

D
dogsled races, 14–15

I
Iditarod Trail, 15
Inuit, 12

L
lead dogs, 21

M
musher, 6, 21, 26–27

N
Nenets, 12

S
Samoyed, 13
Siberian husky, 13
skijoring, 25

T
team, 4, 9, 16, 18–19, 24
team dogs, 18
training, 22, 26

W
wheel dogs, 18

ANSWER KEY:
1. Answers will vary; 2. Answers will vary; 3. A; 4. A; 5. C; 6. C